FOUR CUPS PARTICIPANT'S GUIDE

CHRIS HODGES

PARTICIPANT'S GUIDE

FOUR CUPS

God's Timeless Promises for a Life of Fulfillment

Companion to the *Four Cups DVD Group Experience*

TYNDALE
MOMENTUM

An Imprint of
Tyndale House Publishers, Inc.

Visit Tyndale online at www.tyndale.com.

Visit Tyndale Momentum online at www.tyndalemomentum.com.

TYNDALE, Tyndale Momentum, and the Tyndale Momentum logo are registered trademarks of Tyndale House Publishers, Inc. Tyndale Momentum is an imprint of Tyndale House Publishers, Inc.

Designed by Nicole Grimes

Printed in the United States of America

21 20 19 18 17 16 15
7   6   5   4   3   2   1

TABLE OF CONTENTS

A WORD FROM PASTOR CHRIS HODGES

My journey to understanding the principles of the four cups has changed my life and the way I do ministry. As we share the cups together, I hope it will do the same for you. Four Cups is founded on four foundational promises that God gave us to help us experience life to the fullest: *freedom from sin, deliverance from bondage, purpose for living,* and *a life of joyful abundance.* Symbolized by the four cups used since ancient times in the Jewish celebration of Passover, these four promises still offer us hope today for our deepest thirsts.

No matter where you are on your spiritual journey, you're probably longing for a stronger, deeper faith and a more joyful, purposeful life. The four cups provide the means to fulfill both of those core desires. Each cup reveals God's presence in a distinct and dramatic way. This guide will complement your reading of the book *Four Cups: God's Timeless Promises for a Life of Fulfillment,* enhance your viewing of the *Four Cups DVD Group Experience,* and guide your discussion of the four cups of promise in a group setting.

As we explore the historical background and biblical significance of the four cups, you will gain more than just information. Faith goes beyond an intellectual grasp of a set of facts. It involves *leaning* and *depending* on God and his promises. It is a firm reliance and devoted trust in a *person*—namely, God—and in his ability to do what he says he will do.

Experiencing the four promises that are symbolized in the four cups will draw you closer to God and to your purpose in his Kingdom. Sharing this journey with others will enrich your understanding and encourage you to practice what you've learned.

Are you ready to join me on this journey to discover more about the reality of God's faithfulness? Let's get started. We'll look at how, when, where, and why God made these four timeless promises to his children and at what each one means for you and your life. It's time to drink the "living water" you'll find in each of God's four cups of promise.

HOW TO USE THIS PARTICIPANT'S GUIDE

THE *FOUR CUPS PARTICIPANT'S GUIDE* is a companion to the *Four Cups DVD Group Experience*, an eight-week curriculum designed to deepen your understanding of the four foundational promises of God that are symbolized in the four cups of the Passover celebration. Inspired by the book *Four Cups: God's Timeless Promises for a Life of Fulfillment*, this study was developed to facilitate small-group discussion.

The *Four Cups DVD Group Experience* is based on a transformative sermon series taught by Pastor Chris Hodges at Church of the Highlands in Birmingham, Alabama. Though you can do the study at any time during the year, in the videos you'll journey through the Passover/Easter season at the church, seeing the principles of the *Four Cups* message come to life. As you watch each week, consider how what you're learning applies to your own church. What are you discovering that you can put into practice right now, right where you are?

✳ ✳ ✳

Over the next several weeks, you will gather with your group to study four promises God has made to each one of us. There are eight sessions in this study, each featuring a DVD message from Pastor Chris Hodges. However, the duration of the group experience can be expanded to meet your group's needs. We encourage you to include some fellowship gatherings, where group members can interact beyond the curriculum. For example, here's how you might structure a twelve-week group experience.

Week 1: A "getting to you know you" gathering is a great way to launch a new group. Maybe have a dessert potluck (food is always a good way to make people feel comfortable) and ask some fun icebreaker questions to encourage group members to interact. Review details of the group experience (e.g., what time the group will begin and end, how your group will handle meals or snacks) and encourage group members to think of other friends they can invite to join you. But most important, have fun!

Week 2: Session 1

Week 3: Session 2

Week 4: Session 3

Week 5: Session 4

Week 6: Fellowship Group—This could be a time for group members to have in-depth discussions of ideas and issues raised during the first four weeks, to pray for one another, or simply to socialize and develop group dynamics.

Week 7: Session 5

Week 8: Session 6

Week 9: Session 7

Week 10: Session 8

Week 11: Fellowship Group—Members of the group could share their personal testimonies of what God has done in their lives through this small-group study.

Week 12: Final Meeting—Do something fun with your group to celebrate all that God has done. Some ideas include having a potluck dinner, playing kickball or volleyball, having a game night, or going bowling.

TIPS FOR FINDING NEW MEMBERS FOR YOUR GROUP

Start by praying for God to send people to you whom you haven't yet considered. Think of people who are already in your sphere of influence (coworkers, friends, neighbors). Identify people who are new to the church, who are new believers, or who have shown an interest in getting involved. People often want to get more involved, but they are waiting for someone to invite them. Look for people you can help to draw out their gifts and potential.

SUGGESTED SCHEDULE FOR SMALL GROUP MEETINGS

An hour and fifteen minutes is a good timeframe for group meetings. This allows group members to interact before the meeting begins, while preserving sufficient time for watching the DVD, discussion, and prayer.

1. Fellowship (10 minutes)
2. Just for Fun (5 minutes)
3. Recap and Big Idea (5 minutes)
4. Watch the DVD (20 minutes)
5. Discussion (25 minutes)
6. Prayer (10 minutes)

Remember to start and end on time. Sometimes a vibrant group discussion may cause your meeting to go past your designated ending time. If so, take a quick pause to dismiss the group, so that those who need to leave can do so. Then you can resume the discussion with the group members who want to stay.

WHAT YOU'LL NEED

Before your first meeting, be sure that each group member has a copy of the following three books:

- *Four Cups: God's Timeless Promises for a Life of Fulfillment* by Chris Hodges;
- *Four Cups Participant's Guide*; and
- a Bible.

Also, your group will need a copy of the *Four Cups DVD Group Experience* (available wherever books are sold).

OVERVIEW OF PARTICIPANT'S GUIDE ELEMENTS

Introduction

Each session begins with a brief introduction, which group members will want to read before they arrive for the small-group meeting.

Just for Fun

These icebreaker questions will help get people talking. It is a chance to "warm up" and get to know each other better. Feel free to use the questions provided or come up with your own.

Recap

A short review of the previous week's message.

Big Idea

A single idea that sums up the main point or key idea of the session.

Remember

Each session includes a memory verse to help group members put Colossians 3:16 into action: "Let the message about Christ, in all its richness, fill your lives" (NLT). Scripture renews our minds and transforms our lives. Encourage one another to memorize the verse each week. Convenient memory verse cards are located at the end of this participant's guide.

Watch

We encourage you, as you watch the DVD, to take notes in your participant's guide, filling in the blanks in the outline and writing down any thoughts or questions that come to mind.

Discuss

After you watch the DVD, this is your opportunity to respond to a series of engaging questions designed to encourage discussion and group interaction. Discussing the content of the teaching will help you to understand it better and to begin to live out what you have learned. Your group may not have time to cover every question, and that's okay; ask God to guide your discussion each week, and focus on where he wants you to learn and grow.

Pray

Pray together. In each session, you'll find a suggested prayer focus. Some weeks you may pray in groups of two or three; other times you may close in prayer with the whole group.

For Next Time

Recommended reading in *Four Cups: God's Timeless Promises for a Life of Fulfillment* for group members to complete before the next meeting.

GOD KEEPS HIS PROMISES

Read

Before your group begins the Four Cups small-group study, read chapter 1, "Promises, Promises," in *Four Cups: God's Timeless Promises for a Life of Fulfillment* and answer the following questions:

1. *Pastor Chris talks about Moses and the Promised Land and how God made it clear to his people that he would lead them into a life of freedom. What does "a life of freedom" look like for you today? Do you believe God will lead you there?*

2. *Are you satisfied with where you are in your relationship with God? Or would you like to reach higher ground? How would you define "higher ground" in your spiritual life?*

3. *Pastor Chris describes how, for him, a spiritual journey is like mountain climbing. What have been the recent peaks and valleys in your own journey?*

Introduction

This Four Cups small-group study is based on four unchanging promises that are close to the heart of God. Understanding that these promises are *for you*—and believing in them—is the key to your fulfillment in both this life and the life to come.

When God makes a promise—that is, an offer with a guaranteed result—he always fulfills it. It may not happen the way you want or expect, or in the timing you'd prefer, but God always follows through. When he gives you his word, he keeps it. "God is not a man, so he does not lie. He is not human, so he does not change his mind. Has he ever spoken and failed to act? Has he ever promised and not carried it through?" (Numbers 23:19, NLT).

God wants us to trust him and rely on him. He wants us to live by faith, not by the fulfillment of our own expectations. God wants us to walk with him, trusting him to know what's best for our lives. "His divine power has given us everything we need for a godly life through our knowledge of him who called us by his own glory and goodness. Through these he has given us his very great and precious promises, so that through them you may participate in the divine nature, having escaped the corruption in the world caused by evil desires" (2 Peter 1:3-4, NIV).

The first step in claiming God's promises is simply to study the Bible. God's Word is filled with promises, and you can find one for every trial, challenge, or problem you face.

When life doesn't make sense and you're tempted to doubt God's goodness and sovereignty, you must cling to his promises. That's what it means to trust him and walk by faith, even when you're afraid or when life doesn't make sense, and you can't see where you're going.

In order to activate the power of God's promises, you must pursue him with all your heart. God fulfills his promises in his own way, according to his own all-encompassing wisdom, and in his own time. You may not understand *why* he does what he does or *how* he will accomplish his purposes, but that's why you need to trust him. He wants to teach you, strengthen you, and empower you in ways that only he can. God's promises are foundational to your living by faith and growing in your walk with him.

Just for Fun

What's your favorite beverage? How often have you had it in the past week? Describe the best way to enjoy your favorite drink—with or without ice, glass or go-cup, sugar or no sugar, etc.

Big Idea

More than three thousand years ago, God made some fundamental promises to his people, the Israelites, while they were enslaved in Egypt. These same promises continue to stand today, revealing God's timeless love for all his children. He remains committed to loving, liberating, and leading us in all areas of life—if we'll let him.

Remember

Psalm 138:2 (NLT): "I praise your name for your unfailing love and faithfulness; for your promises are backed by all the honor of your name."

Watch

Watch Session 1, "God Keeps His Promises," on the *Four Cups DVD Group Experience* with Pastor Chris Hodges, and take notes below.

> **2 Peter 1:4 (NIV):** *[God] has given us his very great and precious promises, so that through them you may participate in the divine nature, having escaped the corruption in the world caused by evil desires.*

a) Definition of a Promise: An _____ with a
    _____ result.

> **Joshua 21:45 (NIV):** *Not one of all the LORD's good promises to Israel failed; every one was fulfilled.*

> **Hebrews 6:17-19 (MSG):** *When God wanted to guarantee his promises, he gave his word, a rock-solid guarantee—God can't break his word. And because his word cannot change, the promise is likewise unchangeable. We who have run for our very lives to God have every reason to grab the promised hope with both hands and never let go. It's an unbreakable spiritual lifeline, reaching past all appearances right to the very presence of God.*

b) I need to _____ His promises.

1 Chronicles 17:19 (NLT): *For the sake of your servant, O LORD, and according to your will, you have done all these great things and have made them known.*

c) I need to _____ His promises.

Numbers 23:19 (NLT): *God is not a man, so he does not lie. He is not human, so he does not change his mind. Has he ever spoken and failed to act? Has he ever promised and not carried it through?*

2 Corinthians 1:20 (NLT): *For all of God's promises have been fulfilled in Christ with a resounding "Yes!" And through Christ, our "Amen" (which means "Yes") ascends to God for his glory.*

d) I need to _____ His promises.

Psalm 119:140 (NLT): *Your promises have been thoroughly tested; that is why I love them so much.*

Psalm 119:148 (NIV): *My eyes stay open through the watches of the night, that I may meditate on your promises.*

NOTES

Discuss

1. *Pastor Chris mentions several of the many promises in God's Word that address concerns such as our health, our finances, our relationships, and our peace of mind. What is one promise you're still waiting on God to fulfill? What keeps you going while you wait and how can the group pray for you? What has God taught you in the process of fulfilling his promises?*

2. *Every biblical promise has a premise that requires our participation. In other words, we have to pursue God's promises. How are you pursuing his promises in a specific area of your life right now? What are you doing to facilitate God's participation in your decisions and actions right now?*

3. *How can we keep ourselves (and each other) from falling into a pit of despair—believing lies when we feel as if God hasn't delivered?*

4. *Pastor Chris calls this group adventure a "spiritual maturity" series. In what areas of your life do you hope to grow in maturity through this series?*

Pray

Trust God to meet you exactly where you are and to remind you of his timeless, changeless promises in areas where you are struggling. Lift up in prayer other members of the group and the needs they have. Ask God to provide everyone in the group with the confidence of his peace.

For Next Time

Before the next group meeting, read chapter 2, "Finally Free," in *Four Cups: God's Timeless Promises for a Life of Fulfillment* and answer the following questions:

1. *In this chapter, Pastor Chris describes three "dream killers" that can get in the way of our experiencing God's promises. What are these dream killers, and which one*

*is the biggest challenge for you personally? When do you
typically encounter these dream killers?*

2. *What does Pastor Chris recommend as the way to defeat
these dream killers?*

3. *What is one promise from God that you can cling to
in order to defeat the biggest dream killer in your life?
Where is that promise found?*

GOD'S CORE PROMISES

Introduction

At a dramatic time in Jewish history, when the Israelites were enslaved in Egypt, God made four major promises. God was not about to leave his chosen people enslaved in a foreign land.

Instead, he raised up Moses to lead Israel to a new home: the Promised Land. After a plague-ridden chess game with Pharaoh in which God revealed his power, Moses came to a stalemate with the stubborn leader, who still refused to free the Israelites. So the Lord passed through Egypt, visiting each household—Egyptian and Hebrew alike—and claiming the life of every firstborn male, including the animals.

However, God had told the Israelites that if they painted the doorposts of their homes with the blood of a lamb, the Lord would "pass over" that house and the firstborn would be permitted to live. God made it clear that he would not only spare his people, but he would also lead them to a life of freedom they could not even imagine.

Speaking through Moses, God made the people of Israel four promises (see Exodus 6:6-7):

"I will free you from your oppression."
"I will rescue you from your slavery in Egypt."
"I will redeem you with a powerful arm and great acts of judgment."
"I will claim you as my own people, and I will be your God."

These four "I will" statements became crucial elements of the annual celebration of God's faithfulness known as Passover, which the Jews still observe today. During the main meal of celebration, called the Seder, four cups of wine are used to remember and recognize each of the four promises that God made.

Jesus ultimately fulfilled these four promises and extended God's love and mercy to all people, not just the Israelites. And these promises remain foundational to God's desire to know and love us as his children today. Most believers aren't familiar with the details of the

Passover celebration, but the Seder meal holds the key to what God wants to do in your life right now.

Like the Israelites in Egypt, who waited four hundred years for their liberation, sometimes we have to wait a long time to see God's promises come to fruition. Whether trapped by our circumstances, enslaved by an addiction, or bound by our obligations and responsibilities, we all know what it's like to be held captive by something that restricts our choices and limits our ability to move forward. We call out to God and wonder why he doesn't respond immediately.

In order to experience God's freedom to be who he created us to be, we must overcome three main "dream killers."

First, unfulfilled expectations often limit our faith and prevent us from trusting God with our lives. Next, unrelenting doubts open the door for Satan to undermine our identity and security as God's children. Finally, we must often battle unchangeable circumstances, situations beyond our control that leave us feeling powerless and hopeless. The way to overcome each of these dream killers is the same: claiming God's promise to free us from bondage and liberate us with his love.

Just for Fun

What are your favorite ways to celebrate a special occasion such as a birthday or anniversary? What special foods and activities are a part of your favorite celebrations?

Recap

Last time, we learned that a promise from God is an offer with a guaranteed result. In order to discover and claim God's promises, we must diligently study the Bible. When life doesn't make sense and we're tempted to doubt God's goodness and sovereignty, we must cling to his promises instead. And in order to activate the power of God's promises, we must pursue him with all our hearts.

Big Idea

Of all God's promises, four serve as pillars, supporting all the rest. God first made these promises to the Israelites during their captivity in Egypt in the form of four "I will" statements, revealing how he would rescue them physically, emotionally, psychologically, and spiritually. These same four guarantees still apply today, to you and your future.

Remember

Exodus 6:6-7 (NIV): "I am the LORD, and I will bring you out from under the yoke of the Egyptians. I will free you from being slaves to them, and I will redeem you with an outstretched arm and with mighty acts of judgment. I will take you as my own people, and I will be your God."

Watch

Watch Session 2, "God's Core Promises," on the *Four Cups DVD Group Experience* with Pastor Chris Hodges, and take notes below.

> **Exodus 6:6-7 (NIV):** *Therefore, say to the Israelites: "I am the LORD, and I will bring you out from under the yoke of the Egyptians. I will free you from being slaves to them, and I will redeem you with an outstretched arm and with mighty acts of judgment. I will take you as my own people, and I will be your God. Then you will know that I am the LORD your God, who brought you out from under the yoke of the Egyptians."*

Promise #1: "I will bring you out."

a) God promises me _____.

> **Titus 3:3-8 (MSG):** *It wasn't so long ago that we ourselves were stupid and stubborn, dupes of sin, ordered every which way by our glands, going around with a chip on our shoulder, hated and hating back. But when God, our kind and loving Savior God, stepped in, he saved us from all that. It was all his doing; we had nothing to do with it. He gave us a good bath, and we came out of it new people, washed inside and out by the Holy Spirit. Our Savior Jesus poured*

*out new life so generously. God's gift has restored our
relationship with him and given us back our lives.
And there's more life to come—an eternity of life! You
can count on this.*

Promise #2: "I will free you."

b) God promises me _____.

> **Romans 7:25–8:2 (NIV):** *So then, I myself in my
> mind am a slave to God's law, but in my sinful nature
> a slave to the law of sin. Therefore, there is now no
> condemnation for those who are in Christ Jesus,
> because through Christ Jesus the law of the Spirit who
> gives life has set you free from the law of sin and death.*

Promise #3: "I will redeem you."

c) God promises me _____.

> **Ephesians 1:11-12 (MSG):** *It's in Christ that we
> find out who we are and what we are living for. Long
> before we first heard of Christ and got our hopes up,
> he had his eye on us, had designs on us for glorious
> living, part of the overall purpose he is working out in
> everything and everyone.*

Promise #4: "I will take you as my own people."

d) God promises me _____.

John 10:10 (NIV): *The thief comes only to steal and kill and destroy; I have come that they may have life, and have it to the full.*

NOTES

Discuss

1. *For more than four hundred years, the Israelites waited for God to deliver them from slavery in Egypt. When have you had to wait a long time for God to set you free? Who or what held you captive during this time?*

2. *What did you feel during these times of waiting on God to act? How did you handle these emotions?*

3. *Who serves as a Moses for you when you feel stuck in Egypt? Who are the people God has used in your life to remind you of his truth and to lead you out of bondage?*

4. *Lately, have you seen God doing more to change your circumstances or change what's going on inside your heart? How are the two related?*

5. *Which of God's four key promises intrigues you the most or seems related to where you are in life right now? Which one do you long for the most?*

Pray

Ask God to help you face your dream killers and to help you move forward from the things currently binding you. Share your feelings—including your doubts and fears—with him and ask him to help you trust him fully. Pray for others in your group to grow in their ability to trust him too. Conclude by claiming his promises for your life.

For Next Time

Before the next group meeting, read chapter 3, "Freedom in Christ," in *Four Cups: God's Timeless Promises for a Life of Fulfillment* and answer the following questions:

1. *Throughout the Old Testament, we see the Israelites experience cycles in their relationship with God. They moved from reliance on God's promises to rebellion and*

bondage, requiring God to rescue them over and over again. Describe a time when you've noticed this same pattern (promise/bondage/rescue) in your own life.

2. *How does the Great Commission represent the same four promises that God made to Israel in Exodus 6?*

SESSION 3

CHRIST, OUR PASSOVER LAMB

Introduction

After the Israelites reached the Promised Land, they drifted away from God and worshiped pagan gods and man-made idols. God never gave up on his children, however, and they eventually returned to him—though not for long. Across hundreds of years, they fell into a pattern of living in the truth of God's promises for a while, falling away into sin and bondage, and having to be rescued again by God.

As recorded in the book of Exodus, when God rescued the Israelites from Egypt, he brought judgment on all the people there. In order to protect themselves and avoid the death of their firstborn sons, the Israelites sacrificed perfect, unblemished lambs and smeared the blood on their doorposts. In order to save all of humanity from certain death, God knew he had to take the radical step of sacrificing his Son, Jesus, who would be the ultimate sacrificial lamb. His blood would cleanse God's children from their sins, once and for all.

Jesus fulfilled the requirements set forth in the Old Testament for being a sacrificial lamb. First and foremost, he was *perfect.* "You know that it was not with perishable things such as silver or gold that you were redeemed from the empty way of life handed down to you from your ancestors, but with the precious blood of Christ, a lamb without blemish or defect" (1 Peter 1:18-19, NIV). Only someone who is perfect could save the imperfect. Only someone holy and blameless could take away the sins of the world.

As the Lamb of God, Christ was *slaughtered* and *sacrificed.* Without complaint, he suffered as much as any physical body can endure. Because he endured such intense suffering, we can know peace and healing. "He was pierced for our transgressions, he was crushed for our iniquities; the punishment that brought us peace was on him, and by his wounds we are healed" (Isaiah 53:5, NIV).

As our sacrificial lamb, Jesus must be *shared* with others. Under the law recorded in the Old Testament, the Passover lamb had to be completely consumed. If a household was too small to eat the entire lamb, they shared with another household so that all of the animal would be eaten (see Exodus 12:4). Similarly, Christ died for the sins of everyone, so that we might experience God's grace and know eternal life with him. We must share the good news of the gospel with the people around us, making sure they have the opportunity to experience the feast of the Lamb.

Jesus came to fulfill the promises that God made to his people. And Christ not only fulfilled his Father's promise to free his people from oppression and rescue them from slavery, but he also extended the four cups of promise to all future generations through what has come to be called the Great Commission. He did this by sending his followers to share with all people about his life, death, and resurrection. He promised to never leave them, and he sent the Holy Spirit to lead, comfort, and guide them as they pursued this shared mission.

Just for Fun

If you could excel in one new skill or ability, what would it be? Why would you choose that particular skill or ability?

Recap

When the Israelites, God's chosen people, became enslaved in Egypt, they couldn't imagine how God would honor his promise to free them and lead them to a new home. However, God not only raised up a leader, Moses, to direct their escape from bondage, but he also liberated their minds, hearts, and spirits. He continues to offer us this same liberation if we're willing to rely on him and to trust in his promises.

Big Idea

Fifteen centuries after they left Egypt, the people of Israel still struggled to experience the personal relationship and abundant life that God intended for them. They knew that God had told them to obey his laws, but in their own power they were unable to escape their sinful desires. So God sent Jesus, his only Son, to live as a man, die on the cross, and return to life on the third day. Just as shedding the blood of an unblemished lamb on their doorposts enabled the Israelites to escape death in Egypt, Christ's blood paid the penalty for all the sins of humanity, fulfilling his Father's promise to give his children new life.

Remember

2 Corinthians 1:20 (NLT): "All of God's promises have been fulfilled in Christ with a resounding 'Yes!'"

Watch

Watch Session 3, "Christ: Our Passover Lamb," on the *Four Cups DVD Group Experience* with Pastor Chris Hodges, and take notes below.

Exodus 12:26-27 (NIV): *When your children ask you, "What does this ceremony mean to you?" then tell them, "It is the Passover sacrifice to the LORD, who passed over the houses of the Israelites in Egypt and spared our homes when he struck down the Egyptians."*

Luke 22:15-16, 19-20 (NIV): *He said to them, "I have eagerly desired to eat this Passover with you before I suffer. For I tell you, I will not eat it again until it finds fulfillment in the kingdom of God." . . . And he took bread, gave thanks and broke it, and gave it to them, saying, "This is my body given for you; do this in remembrance of me." In the same way, after the supper he took the cup, saying, "This cup is the new covenant in my blood, which is poured out for you."*

1 Corinthians 5:7 (NLT): *Christ, our Passover Lamb, has been sacrificed for us.*

John 1:29 (NLT): *The next day John saw Jesus coming toward him and said, "Look! The Lamb of God who takes away the sin of the world!"*

a) The Lamb was _____.

Exodus 12:5 (NIV): *The animals you choose must be year-old males without defect, and you may take them from the sheep or the goats.*

1 Peter 1:18-19 (NIV): *You were redeemed . . . with the precious blood of Christ, a lamb without blemish or defect.*

b) The Lamb was _____.

Exodus 12:6 (NIV): *Take care of them [the animals] until the fourteenth day of the month, when all the people of the community of Israel must slaughter them at twilight.*

Isaiah 53:5 (NIV): *He was pierced for our transgressions, he was crushed for our iniquities; the punishment that brought us peace was on him, and by his wounds we are healed.*

c) The Lamb was _____.

Exodus 12:4 (NIV): *If any household is too small for a whole lamb, they must share one with their nearest neighbor.*

2 Corinthians 5:19 (NIV): *God was reconciling the world to himself in Christ, not counting people's sins against them. And he has committed to us the message of reconciliation.*

NOTES

Discuss

1. *How has your dependence on God or your nearness to him affected your perspective on your life's circumstances?*

2. *We all experience difficult seasons in life. When have you been forced to rely on God to rescue you from hard times,*

painful emotions, and challenging obstacles? How did
you experience his presence in your life then?

3. *When Jesus was born, the nation of Israel was suffering*
   under Roman rule. Aware of God's promises from
   generations past, including the promise for a Messiah
   to liberate them once again, the Jews expected Christ to
   be a revolutionary who would wage a triumphant war
   on the Roman Empire. They were not prepared for a
   carpenter from Nazareth—a teacher who mingled with
   fishermen, tax collectors, and prostitutes—to be their
   Savior. What was your understanding of Jesus while
   you were growing up? Who or what contributed to this
   impression that you formed of him? Looking back, how
   accurately did you understand Jesus' role in your life?

4. *Pastor Chris emphasizes three distinct ways that Jesus becomes the Lamb of God. First, he's perfect and free from sin. He suffered all the same temptations that you face without giving in to them. Second, he suffered and died so that the penalty for your sin would be paid once and for all. Finally, he came for all people, not just his followers in Israel during his lifetime. Jesus sent the Holy Spirit to dwell in us so that we could live a fulfilled, purposeful life as we share this good news with others. How would you explain Jesus' role as the Lamb of God to someone unfamiliar with Scripture?*

5. *What are some past ways you've shared the good news about Jesus with others? How are you currently sharing the gospel with other people?*

Pray

Thank God for desiring to have such a close, loving relationship with you. Let him know how grateful you are for the ways he has rescued you in the past by providing for your needs, healing your wounds, and delivering you from danger. Most of all, thank him for the amazing gift of his Son, Jesus Christ, the perfect Lamb, who suffered and died and rose again to pay the price for your sins.

For Next Time

Before the next group meeting, read chapter 4, "The Cup of Sanctification," in *Four Cups: God's Timeless Promises for a Life of Fulfillment* and answer the following questions:

1. *Many people seem to assume that sanctification means "righteousness" or "perfection." But that isn't true. What does it actually mean to be sanctified? How has God sanctified you?*

2. In this chapter, Pastor Chris writes, "God put you on planet Earth at this exact time and place so that you can fulfill the purpose for which you were created." Do you know what your true purpose is? What has God uniquely designed you to do in this life?

3. What is God's first promise, which is associated with the Cup of Sanctification? Do you believe that God can bring you out of whatever circumstance you're currently struggling with? What is your role in that deliverance?

SESSION 4

THE CUP OF SANCTIFICATION

Introduction

When God promised the Israelites, "I will bring you out from under the yoke of the Egyptians" (Exodus 6:6, NIV), he kept his word—even when Pharaoh tried to stand in the way. During the Passover celebration, Jews still celebrate the time when God redeemed them out of slavery in Egypt. The first cup in the Seder celebration symbolizes God's promise to save his people so they can live new lives of freedom, the lives he always intended for them.

God's desire to free his people from bondage remains at the center of his work in the world. He makes the same promise to us today by providing a way out of our bondage to sin through the power of his Son. We are no longer enslaved to sin. We can now live in the freedom that comes from making Christ our Savior and the Lord of our lives.

You may find yourself in some type of bondage right now. It could be an addiction or a secret habit that you cling to. It could be an unhealthy relationship or an obsession with appearing successful in the eyes of others. Maybe you started a relationship with God in the past and you've drifted away. Maybe you want to change, but you aren't sure how to get started.

Regardless of what entangles you, the freedom that comes from the Cup of Sanctification begins when you invite God into your heart. It isn't until God begins working in your life that change can take place. Once he has found a home in your heart and becomes Lord of your life, both the *desire* to change and the *power* to change start working in your life.

No matter where you are in your relationship with God, he will never give up on you or abandon you. God is always pursuing you. He has never stopped thinking about you. He has seen your wandering and your suffering, and he wants you to come back to him. Your Father wants to lead you out of your particular Egypt, whatever it may be; all you have to do is follow him.

So how do you drink from the Cup of Sanctification? In a word: *surrender*. When you follow someone, you give up control over where you're going and trust that your leader knows the way. Give up control of your life; give it to God. He sees your bondage and has sent his only Son to set you free. All you have to do is follow him. If you have never made Jesus the Lord of your life, or if you've wandered far from God, he's waiting to lead you to new heights of freedom, purpose, and fulfillment.

Just for Fun

What special item, such as your father's watch or your wedding china, have you set aside to use or wear only on holidays and other milestone events? How often do you use this item? When was the last time?

Recap

Just as the blood of an unblemished lamb on their door-posts enabled the Israelites to escape death in Egypt, Christ's blood paid the penalty for all the sins of humanity, fulfilling his Father's promise to give his children new life. The four key promises God made at Passover are fulfilled in the life, death, and resurrection of his Son.

Big Idea

Sanctification means "to be set apart as special and holy to God"; it doesn't mean we have to be perfect. Though we're not slaves in Egypt, we all struggle with the yoke of bondage from our sinful nature. However, Christ sets us free from this great burden that would otherwise separate us from God forever. Through Jesus, we can have a personal relationship with our Father, set apart as his people who will someday spend eternity with him in heaven.

Remember

Titus 3:4-5 (NIV): "When the kindness and love of God our Savior appeared, he saved us, not because of righteous things we had done, but because of his mercy."

Watch

Watch Session 4, "The Cup of Sanctification," on the *Four Cups DVD Group Experience* with Pastor Chris Hodges, and take notes below.

> **Exodus 6:6-7 (NIV):** *I will bring you out from under the yoke of the Egyptians. I will free you from being slaves to them, and I will redeem you with an outstretched arm and with mighty acts of judgment. I will take you as my own people, and I will be your God. Then you will know that I am the LORD your God, who brought you out from under the yoke of the Egyptians.*

> **John 10:10 (NIV):** *The thief comes only to steal and kill and destroy; I have come that they may have life, and have it to the full.*

Romans 8:11 (MSG): *It stands to reason, doesn't it, that if the alive-and-present God who raised Jesus from the dead moves into your life, he'll do the same thing in you that he did in Jesus, bringing you alive to himself? When God lives and breathes in you . . . , you are delivered from that dead life. With his Spirit living in you, your body will be as alive as Christ's!*

1 Peter 1:3-4 (MSG): *Because Jesus was raised from the dead, we've been given a brand-new life and have everything to live for, including a future in heaven—and the future starts now!*

a) Make the move: _____.

2 Corinthians 6:17-18 (NIV): *Therefore, "Come out from them and be separate, says the Lord. Touch no unclean thing, and I will receive you." And, "I will be a Father to you, and you will be my sons and daughters, says the Lord Almighty."*

b) Let it go: _____.

Mark 8:34-35 (MSG): *Anyone who intends to come with me has to let me lead. You're not in the driver's seat; I am. . . . Follow me and I'll show you how. Self-help is no help at all. Self-sacrifice is the way, my way, to saving yourself.*

c) Commit your life: _____.

Romans 6:19 (NIV): *Just as you used to offer yourselves as slaves to impurity and to ever-increasing wickedness, so now offer yourselves as slaves to righteousness leading to holiness.*

NOTES

Discuss

1. *Pastor Chris shares three simple steps to help us quench our thirst for freedom in the Cup of Sanctification. First, we must choose to follow God and make the move. We must change the direction we've been going and allow God to lead us instead. Next, we must let go*

*of the things we've been carrying. We must surrender
and acknowledge that we cannot escape the bondage
of sin on our own. Finally, we must commit our lives
to a relationship with God and dedicate our energies
to serving him and living out the purpose he has for
us. From your experience, which of these three steps
has been the hardest or most challenging—choosing to
change course, surrendering certain areas of your life, or
committing to a real relationship with God? Why?*

2. *What's an area of your life God wants you to surrender
to him right now? Why is it so hard to let go of this area?*

3. *How would you describe your relationship with God
presently? Close? Distant? Friendly? Uncertain? Loving?
Uncomfortable? Intimate? How would you like your
relationship with God to be? What do you need to do*

in order to draw closer to him and pursue this kind of relationship?

4. *How can we help one another take the necessary steps to follow God, leave "Egypt" behind, and step into the new life that God intends for us?*

5. *What was the turning point when you were ready to surrender and follow God? How did you get out of bondage? Who, or what, helped you to repent—to literally change direction in your life? Or do you feel as if you're still in the process of leaving Egypt?*

Pray

Thank God for loving you so much and for never giving up on you, no matter what you've done or not done, no matter where you are in life right now. Thank him for the gift of salvation that he's promised you through Christ's death and resurrection, the sacrifice that paid for your sins and freed you from captivity. If you haven't accepted this free gift, receiving what Jesus did for you on the cross, then ask him to be your Savior and the Lord of your life. If you have already received this wonderful gift, then praise him for the ways he continues to set you free.

For Next Time

Before the next group meeting, read chapter 5, "The Cup of Deliverance," in *Four Cups: God's Timeless Promises for a Life of Fulfillment* and answer the following questions:

1. *Pastor Chris says that 80 to 90 percent of Christians need to drink from the Cup of Deliverance. Do you feel trapped in your old life? What would deliverance look like in your life?*

2. *How do we allow God's Spirit to transform us into truly free people?*

3. *What is the role of confession in our receiving of God's promised Cup of Deliverance?*

SESSION 5

THE CUP OF DELIVERANCE

Introduction

The desire to free his people from bondage remains at the center of God's heart. For the Israelites this happened literally, when God delivered them from captivity in Egypt. However, once they were free, the people were so accustomed to slavery that they continued to think and act like slaves. They rebelled against God's ways, created idols, and worshiped pagan gods.

We often have a similar mind-set and do the same kinds of things—even after we've given our lives to God and welcomed his Holy Spirit into our hearts. We may know that we're saved, but we struggle with changing our sinful thought patterns and behaviors. Many believers are on their way to heaven, but here on earth they remain plagued by sinful habits, secret addictions, and selfish attitudes.

In order to move into the future God has for you, your mind and actions must align with your commitment to Christ. Salvation, which we linked to the Cup of Sanctification, begins the process of your spiritual transformation as your spirit becomes renewed and recalibrated to God's original purpose. As you submit to the power of the Holy Spirit in your life, your body and soul go through a cleansing process. Rather than continuing in the sinful ways that had become your default mode, you learn new ways that please God.

In order to drink from the Cup of Deliverance and experience this kind of realignment, you need help from other believers who are committed to obeying God and his guidelines just as much as you are. When you struggle with old ways of thinking and acting, you can help each other, reminding and encouraging one another to stay focused on God's way and not your own. By holding one another accountable to God's standards, confessing to one another, and asking for help when you need it, you change your default setting of selfish sinfulness.

When you focus on specific areas of your life in community with other Christians, you begin to change old thoughts and to choose new behaviors. Specifically, you need to look at your addictions (defined as any person, substance, object, or activity that has power over you), past wounds, and present areas of weakness. God wants to set you free to enjoy an abundant life of purpose, peace, and passionate service for his Kingdom. The devil, however, wants to play target practice with your attempts to change. He wants you to fail and to remain trapped in the bondage of sinful thoughts and harmful behavior, even after your salvation is secured.

But God is greater and more powerful than anything the enemy can throw at you. Your Father has promised to liberate you, not just from your sinful nature but also from the sinful thoughts and actions left over from before you were saved. He knows what's best for you and wants you to experience life to the fullest. True freedom—in spirit, mind, and body—is yours in the Cup of Deliverance.

Just for Fun

It's often fun to look back and remember times from the past. What's one of your favorite old movies? When was the last time you watched it? What's one thing you love about it?

Recap

At Passover, the Cup of Sanctification reminds participants of the way God freed the people of Israel from Egyptian slavery. Similarly, he has freed us from bondage to our sinful nature, through the gift of salvation made possible by Christ's death on the cross and his resurrection to new life. When we receive this gift and drink from the Cup of Sanctification, we begin a personal relationship with God and are set apart as his people.

Big Idea

After the Israelites escaped from Egypt, they still struggled with thinking and acting like slaves. The Cup of Deliverance represents how God also liberated their thoughts and behavior; they no longer had to think or act like slaves. Through our salvation, God gives us this same liberating promise. After we're saved and sanctified, we often continue to struggle with sinful habits, painful wounds from our past, and secret addictions—but we don't have to. When we taste the Cup of Deliverance, we experience a new mind-set and divine power to live fully in the freedom of Christ.

Remember

Romans 7:24-25 (NLT): "Who will free me from this life that is dominated by sin and death? Thank God! The answer is in Jesus Christ our Lord."

Watch

Watch Session 5, "The Cup of Deliverance," on the *Four Cups DVD Group Experience* with Pastor Chris Hodges, and take notes below.

Ephesians 2:8-9 (NLT): *God saved you by his grace when you believed. And you can't take credit for this; it is a gift from God. Salvation is not a reward for the good things we have done, so none of us can boast about it.*

Philippians 2:12-13 (NLT): *Work hard to show the results of your salvation, obeying God with deep reverence and fear. For God is working in you, giving you the desire and the power to do what pleases him.*

a) Victory over _____.

Romans 7:21-25 (NIV): *I find this law at work: Although I want to do good, evil is right there with me. For in my inner being I delight in God's law; but I see another law at work in me, waging war against the law of my mind and making me a prisoner of the law of sin at work within me. What a wretched man I am! Who will rescue me from this body that is subject to death? Thanks be to God, who delivers me through Jesus Christ our Lord!*

b) Healing from _____.

Ephesians 4:26-27 (NLT): *And "don't sin by letting anger control you." Don't let the sun go down while you are still angry, for anger gives a foothold to the devil.*

c) Authority over the _____.

Romans 8:1-2 (NLT): *So now there is no condemnation for those who belong to Christ Jesus. And because you belong to him, the power of the life-giving Spirit has freed you from the power of sin that leads to death.*

Romans 8:5-6 (NLT): *Those who are dominated by the sinful nature think about sinful things, but those who are controlled by the Holy Spirit think about things that please the Spirit. So letting your sinful nature control your mind leads to death. But letting the Spirit control your mind leads to life and peace.*

Ephesians 6:10-12 (NIV): *Be strong in the Lord and in his mighty power. Put on the full armor of God, so that you can take your stand against the devil's schemes. For our struggle is not against flesh and blood, but against the rulers, against the authorities, against the powers of this dark world and against the spiritual forces of evil in the heavenly realms.*

d) _____ are the key.

Proverbs 28:13 (NIV): *Whoever conceals their sins does not prosper, but the one who confesses and renounces them finds mercy.*

James 5:16 (NIV): *Therefore confess your sins to each other and pray for each other so that you may be healed.*

1 John 1:9 (NIV): *If we confess our sins, he is faithful and just and will forgive us our sins and purify us from all unrighteousness.*

NOTES

Discuss

1. *Often when we attempt to change bad habits, we try to eliminate them by sheer willpower. Whether it's more time with family, increased exercise, or overcoming an addiction, we can never truly change without God's power in our lives. When have you attempted to kick*

*a bad habit in your own power? How did the way you
thought about this habit hinder your attempts?*

2. *Anything other than God that holds sway over our
   hearts becomes an idol. Where are you currently in your
   battle with idols? How can others help you experience
   the freedom God promised in the Cup of Deliverance?*

3. *Why is confessing our sins to one another so important
   to this internal process of change? Why is it so difficult at
   times? What prevents us from "being real" and confessing
   our sins to one another more often?*

Pray

Welcome God's healing presence and transforming power into your heart as you seek to align your thoughts, words, and actions with your commitment to him. Confess your sins to God and thank him for being faithful to forgive you and cleanse you from all unrighteousness. Let him know how much you want to change the sinful thought patterns or behaviors in your life. Ask him to give you the courage and wisdom to approach other believers with whom you can share your struggles and confess your sins. Thank him for what he's doing in your life right now and where he's leading you.

For Next Time

Before the next group meeting, read chapter 6, "The Cup of Redemption," in *Four Cups: God's Timeless Promises for a Life of Fulfillment* and answer the following questions:

1. *In this chapter, Pastor Chris says that "redemption is the essence of discipleship." What does this mean, and how does viewing discipleship as redemptive help us in our relationships with other people?*

2. *Pastor Chris shares that he almost missed God's purpose for his life because he failed to see the potential in his abilities. Who in your life can "be your eyes," helping to spot areas of strength in your character? How can you be the "eyes" for someone else?*

3. *The apostle Paul's ministry illustrates the need for focus in our drinking from the Cup of Redemption. Where is your focus currently? How can you shift your focus to the Lord and his desires for your life?*

SESSION 6

THE CUP OF REDEMPTION

Introduction

To *redeem* simply means to buy back something or to cash in its value in order to receive something else. It also means to win back; to free something from what distresses or harms it; to liberate someone from captivity by paying a ransom; to reform and restore. As with all of God's promises represented by the four cups, Jesus fulfills the Cup of Redemption. Through his death on the cross, he paid the debt of our sin—a debt we could never pay on our own. In return for our redemption, we can be the people that God created us to be and live out of our unique, God-given purpose.

What does it mean to live out of your purpose? It means that God had a specific, unique function in mind when he designed you. He made you exactly the way you are so that you can do what you're called to do. And when you do what you were born to do, it brings incredible satisfaction, peace, and a natural sense of passion to get up in the morning and serve others with your personal contribution.

In the church, we usually call this special, individual purpose a *spiritual gift*, which simply means that it's God-given and empowered by the Holy Spirit. For some people, it's the gift of hospitality: serving others by preparing meals, offering accommodations, and hosting events. For others, it's the gift of worship through their musical and vocal talent. Maybe it's the spiritual gift of leadership, or teaching, or mercy. "We have different gifts, according to the grace given to each of us" (Romans 12:6, NIV).

Once you discover how God designed you to serve, it's important to develop your gift. Usually, this occurs within the relationships of your church, small group, or other Christian community. As you commit yourself to participate in the body of Christ and obey God's instructions, you will begin to understand your talents and abilities and can practice serving God by serving others.

The Cup of Redemption is about discovering your true identity and living out of your divine purpose. Drinking from this cup produces a contentment that no amount of money or personal achievement can ever provide. Knowing what you were born to do, you can then give

God your best, even as you experience the satisfaction of serving others with your unique abilities, talents, and spiritual gifts.

Just for Fun

Using a coupon provides a good picture of redemption— when you redeem a coupon, you receive its value. How often do you use coupons? What's the best deal you've ever gotten using a coupon?

Recap

After God delivered the Israelites from slavery in Egypt, they still struggled with thinking and acting like slaves. So God promised to deliver them from their old way of thinking so they could fully enjoy their freedom, just as he intended. He promises us the same kind of liberation. Through the power of the Holy Spirit—symbolized by the Cup of Deliverance in the Passover celebration—we can experience a new mind-set and divine power to live fully in the freedom of Christ.

Big Idea

God was not only interested in saving and delivering the people of Israel from slavery, but he also had a bigger plan for them. He wanted to redeem their past suffering by transforming them into people who would live lives of freedom and purpose. God promises to do the same for us. The Cup of Redemption means that God enables us to do what we were created to do.

Remember

Ephesians 2:10 (NIV): "For we are God's handiwork, created in Christ Jesus to do good works, which God prepared in advance for us to do."

Watch

Watch Session 6, "The Cup of Redemption," on the *Four Cups DVD Group Experience* with Pastor Chris Hodges, and take notes below.

> **Romans 12:6 (NIV):** *We have different gifts, according to the grace given to each of us.*

> **1 Corinthians 14:1 (NIV):** *Follow the way of love and eagerly desire gifts of the Spirit.*

a) _____ your gift.

> **Psalm 139:13-14 (NLT):** *You made all the delicate, inner parts of my body and knit me together in my mother's womb. Thank you for making me*

so wonderfully complex! Your workmanship is marvelous—how well I know it.

Colossians 1:16 (MSG): *For everything, absolutely everything, above and below, visible and invisible . . . everything got started in him and finds its purpose in him.*

b) _____ your gift.

Ephesians 4:7, 11-12 (NIV): *To each one of us grace has been given as Christ apportioned it. . . . So Christ himself gave the apostles, the prophets, the evangelists, the pastors and teachers, to equip his people for works of service, so that the body of Christ may be built up.*

c) _____ your gift.

Hebrews 6:10 (NIV): *God is not unjust; he will not forget your work and the love you have shown him as you have helped his people and continue to help them.*

1 Peter 4:10 (NLT): *God has given each of you a gift from his great variety of spiritual gifts. Use them well to serve one another.*

d) My purpose is to _____ by _____.

NOTES

Discuss

1. *Terms such as redemption and spiritual gifts
   sound theological and "churchy." But in the Cup
   of Redemption you can see how intertwined these
   two concepts are. Because God has designed us for a
   specific purpose, he can transform any and all of our
   experiences to help us live out our destiny. It may
   appear to be a crisis, disappointment, or mistake to
   us at the time, but later we can often see God's hand
   at work. How has God redeemed your past mistakes
   or painful past experiences? How have you learned*

to help others through what you've learned and what you've seen God redeem in your life?

2. *What experiences or individuals have helped you discern your God-given purpose in life? Do you feel like you're living out your purpose by what you're doing presently? What barriers make it challenging for you to live out your purpose?*

3. *How confident are you that you know your spiritual gifts? What are they? How did you discover them?*

4. *How have you been able to use your spiritual gifts to serve others? How do you feel when you're serving others by sharing your spiritual gifts?*

5. *Who has blessed you through their service to you and others this past week?*

Pray

Thank God for designing you with a custom-made purpose long before you were ever born. Tell him how much you appreciate the gifts you've been given so that you can serve others. Ask him to open your eyes so that you can see yourself for who you truly are, just as he sees you. Pray for the wisdom and discernment necessary to discover, develop, and live out the redemptive plan God has for your life. Commit to serve him with every ounce of your being—mind, body, and soul. Close by praying for the needs of others in the group.

For Next Time

Before the next group meeting, read chapter 7, "The Cup of Praise," in *Four Cups: God's Timeless Promises for a Life of Fulfillment* and answer the following questions:

1. *Pastor Chris conveys how one of his "heroes in ministry," Pastor Tommy Barnett, replied to the question, "Do you have any regrets? Anything you wish you'd done differently in your life?" Pastor Barnett's response? "I wish I would have dreamed bigger. And I wish I would have risked more." In what areas of your life do you need to dream bigger and risk more in order to live a life without regrets?*

2. *Where would you place yourself on Maslow's hierarchy of needs? What would it take to move you up to*

the next level? What obstacles hinder your pursuit
of transcendence?

3. *Pastor Chris says that "the happiest people on the planet*
   are those who are making a difference in the lives of
   other people." Who are some of the happiest people
   you know? What sets them apart from the rest of your
   friends?

SESSION 7

THE CUP OF PRAISE

Introduction

The Cup of Praise is the culmination of the three cups that precede it. In the original Passover ceremony, the fourth cup—or the *hallel* (from which we get our word *hallelujah*), as it's called—celebrated God's promise to restore Israel as a nation in a new home, the Promised Land. They knew that God had blessed them and set them apart, and they praised him for giving them a fulfilled life, a purposeful place in the world.

When we experience the fulfillment of God's abundance in our lives, we naturally experience this same desire to praise and celebrate what he's done for us. We're not only saved through the price paid by Christ on the cross;

we're not only empowered and freed from the power of sin in our lives; we're not only redeemed by living out our purpose in the world. We're part of something bigger.

God's ultimate plan is for you to be both *full* and *filled*, encompassing the two roots of the word *fulfilled*. When we experience life at its best by living out our purposeful identity, we feel such joy, peace, and contentment that we love waking up every morning. We love life because we know why we are here and what we have to offer. Greater still, we know we're not alone, that we're united in the body of Christ with brothers and sisters of kindred spirit. We know that we're living life to the fullest and accomplishing a positive purpose for eternity.

You may not see yourself as a world changer, but that's how God sees you. The satisfaction you're looking for in life comes from being in the middle of the action, not on the sidelines. When you discover your calling, develop its potential, and use it to serve others, you change the world. Everyone is called to minister, not just preachers and people in vocational ministry. There's no better feeling than when you're serving God in whatever unique capacity he's created you to serve, and you can say, "I was made for this!"

It gets even better, because we know we're not alone in our goal to love God and serve his Kingdom. We know we're doing our part alongside other brothers and sisters in the body of Christ. We all have different gifts and roles for serving, but we all work together toward something greater than anything we can do as individuals. God made us to be relational beings in community with others. And when we invest in one another's lives and accomplish God's goals together, we also get to celebrate together. We all share in the goodness of the Lord and praise him for our many blessings. This is what the Cup of Praise is all about.

Just for Fun

In chapter 7 of *Four Cups: God's Timeless Promises for a Life of Fulfillment*, Pastor Chris mentions his "bucket list"—things he wants to do before he dies. Share some of the things that are on your own bucket list.

Recap

In addition to delivering the Israelites from slavery, God also had a bigger plan in mind for his people. He wanted to transform their lives into lives of freedom and purpose. He has promised to do the same for us today. When we drink from the Cup of Redemption, we discover what we were created to do, and we use our gifts to serve God's Kingdom.

Big Idea

The Jews call the fourth cup of Passover *hallel*, a word that means to boast, rave about, praise, and celebrate. Commemorating the Exodus from Egypt, they rejoice in the way God freed them, saved them, redeemed them, and fulfilled them. We, too, can know this kind of contentment as we live out the purpose for which we were created. As a part of God's family, we are his beloved children who serve his Kingdom, knowing we're part of something bigger than ourselves and working alongside others to fulfill God's plan.

Remember

John 10:10 (TLB): "The thief's purpose is to steal, kill, and destroy. My purpose is to give life in all its fullness."

Watch

Watch Session 7, "The Cup of Praise," on the *Four Cups DVD Group Experience* with Pastor Chris Hodges, and take notes below.

> **Exodus 6:7 (NIV):** *I will take you as my own people, and I will be your God.*

> **Ecclesiastes 4:8 (NIV):** *There was a man all alone; he had neither son nor brother. There was no end to his toil, yet his eyes were not content with his wealth.*

a) It begins with a _____.

> **2 Timothy 1:9 (MSG):** *[God] first saved us and then called us to this holy work. We had nothing to do with*

it. It was all his idea, a gift prepared for us in Jesus long before we knew anything about it.

b) _____ make a difference.

c) It stands on a _____.

Acts 20:24 (NLT): *My life is worth nothing to me unless I use it for finishing the work assigned me by the Lord Jesus—the work of telling others the Good News about the wonderful grace of God.*

d) _____ that makes a difference.

e) It spreads from _____.

Ecclesiastes 4:9 (NIV): *Two are better than one, because they have a good return for their labor.*

f) _____ who want to make a difference.

Matthew 26:26-29 (NIV): *While they were eating, Jesus took bread, and when he had given thanks, he broke it and gave it to his disciples, saying, "Take and eat; this is my body." Then he took a cup, and when he had given thanks, he gave it to them, saying, "Drink from it, all of you. . . . I tell you, I will not drink from this fruit of the vine from now on until that day when I drink it new with you in my Father's kingdom."*

John 15:8-11 (NIV): *This is to my Father's glory, that you bear much fruit, showing yourselves to be my disciples. As the Father has loved me, so have I loved you. Now remain in my love. If you keep my commands, you will remain in my love, just as I have kept my Father's commands and remain in his love. I have told you this so that my joy may be in you and that your joy may be complete.*

g) Jesus himself will _____ with you and me.

Revelation 19:9 (NIV): *Blessed are those who are invited to the wedding supper of the Lamb!*

NOTES

Discuss

1. *The Cup of Praise touches our deepest longings and desires to live life on a large scale, enjoying all of God's blessings as we live out his purpose for our lives in community with others. In fact, psychologists studying human needs over time have documented that, in addition to physical, emotional, and cognitive needs, we also instinctively crave transcendence. We not only want to be living out our full potential, but we also want to leave a legacy, knowing that we've made a difference. Based on where you are in life right now, do you feel as if your need for transcendence is being met? How close have you come to experiencing this sense of joyful, purposeful fulfillment in your life? What are some practical steps you can take to start living your dream?*

2. *What challenges often keep you from experiencing this life of fulfillment God wants you to live? How do you usually respond to these barriers?*

3. *What kind of legacy would you like to leave? What difference do you hope to make in the lives of those around you?*

4. *What goal or specific cause would you like to pursue with other similar-minded believers? What specific mission, cause, or ministry stirs your heart and fits with your calling and spiritual gifting?*

5. *Who are some of the significant people in your life who have had an eternal impact on you by the way they have loved, challenged, or encouraged you? What would you like to say to them if given the opportunity?*

Pray

Spend some time thanking and praising God for designing you to live life to the fullest. Name some of the specific people in your life for whom you are especially thankful right now. Thank God for his goodness in your life, as demonstrated by his many blessings. Ask him to give you a renewed sense of commitment to serving out your calling, knowing you're part of something bigger, making a difference in the lives of others for eternity.

For Next Time

Before the next group meeting, read the Afterword, "A Model for Church Leaders," in *Four Cups: God's Timeless Promises for a Life of Fulfillment* and answer the following questions:

1. *Pastor Chris says that he measures success at Church of the Highlands "when people are moving from where they are to where God wants them to be." How is success defined in your congregation? In light of what you've learned by reading* Four Cups: God's Timeless Promises for a Life of Fulfillment *and participating in the* Four Cups DVD Group Experience, *what changes (if any) would you make to your definition of success?*

2. *How would you apply each cup at your church?*

Cup of Salvation

Cup of Deliverance

Cup of Redemption

Cup of Praise

SESSION 8

CELEBRATING THE JOURNEY

Introduction

Everyone is on a spiritual journey. No matter where you are along the way—whether you've been a follower of Jesus for most of your life, you've just recently invited him into your heart, or you're somewhere in between—you long for more. Maybe you're in survival mode, just trying to keep your head above water by holding down your job, paying the bills, and providing for your family. Maybe you're in a rut—your faith used to be vibrant but now feels kind of stale. Maybe you're experiencing wonderful joy on your journey with God but wish you knew how to share it with others more effectively.

Regardless of where you find yourself, you're not alone

in wanting to know how to move forward. We all want to know where we are, where we're going, and how we're going to get there. We want to be empowered for the journey of life; to be equipped by God so we can do more than just survive; and to experience the abundant joy, peace, and satisfaction that he promised.

Though it's tempting to think that understanding this process of development means obeying a bunch of rules and guidelines, it's really much simpler than that. As you have learned with your group these past few weeks, God's love for us comes into sharper focus when we look at the key promises he made to the people of Israel thousands of years ago.

Enslaved in Egypt at the time, the Israelites received four promises from God:

1. "I will free you from your oppression."
2. "I will rescue you from your slavery in Egypt."
3. "I will redeem you with a powerful arm and great acts of judgment."
4. "I will claim you as my own people, and I will be your God."

"Then," God concluded, "you will know that I am the LORD your God who has freed you from your oppression in Egypt" (Exodus 6:6-7, NLT).

These four "I will" statements were foundational for the nation of Israel and became crucial elements of the annual celebration of God's faithfulness known as

Passover, which they still observe today. At this yearly event, four cups of wine are used to remember the four promises that God made. These four cups of promise, as they're called, bridge the gap between ancient history, our present day, and the future. For Jewish families, it's like celebrating Independence Day, a time to remember when God brought them out of slavery and into freedom, redemption, and fulfillment.

The four cups hold the same promise for all of us today. If a promise is an offer with a guaranteed result, one that often begins with a declaration of what one person will do for another, then the four cups of promise reveal what God will do for us if we let him. No matter where you may be on your spiritual journey right now, these promises hold the key to what God wants to do in your life.

Just for Fun

Many Jews still observe Passover, along with other cultural holidays such as Yom Kippur and Hanukkah, as a way of honoring God and celebrating their Jewish heritage. How do you keep your family's culture alive? What traditions or holidays do you and your family celebrate each year?

Recap

Commemorating the Exodus from Egypt, the Jews use the fourth cup at Passover, called the *hallel*, to celebrate how

God freed them, saved them, redeemed them, and fulfilled them. As part of God's family, we also share in the Cup of Praise as we use our gifts, talents, and abilities to fulfill the purpose for which we were created. We're united with other believers, together accomplishing an eternal legacy as we share the good news of the gospel.

Big Idea

God remains constant in his timeless purpose to rescue, redeem, and love his people. This commitment started with Adam and Eve in the Garden of Eden, continued with the people of Israel across thousands of years, and found fulfillment in the precious sacrifice of God's only Son, Jesus. God's foundational promises to his people have remained the same, and the four cups used to celebrate the Jewish holiday of Passover symbolize the gifts he still offers to people today: salvation, freedom, redemption, and fulfillment.

Remember

Ephesians 1:11-12 (MSG): "It's in Christ that we find out who we are and what we are living for. Long before we first heard of Christ and got our hopes up, he had his eye on us, had designs on us for glorious living, part of the overall purpose he is working out in everything and everyone."

Watch

Watch Session 8, "Celebrating the Journey," on the *Four Cups DVD Group Experience* with Pastor Chris Hodges, and take notes below.

> **Ephesians 1:11-12 (MSG):** *It's in Christ that we find out who we are and what we are living for. Long before we first heard of Christ and got our hopes up, he had his eye on us, had designs on us for glorious living, part of the overall purpose he is working out in everything and everyone.*

a) Be _____ and _____.

> **John 8:34 (NIV):** *Jesus replied, "Very truly I tell you, everyone who sins is a slave to sin."*

> **Titus 3:3-7 (MSG):** *It wasn't so long ago that we ourselves were stupid and stubborn, dupes of sin, ordered every which way by our glands, going around with a chip on our shoulder, hated and hating back. But when God, our kind and loving Savior God, stepped in, he saved us from all that. It was all his doing; we had nothing to do with it. He gave us a good bath, and we came out of it new people, washed inside and out by the Holy Spirit. Our Savior Jesus poured out new life so generously. God's gift has restored our relationship with him and given us back our lives. And there's more life to come—an eternity of life!*

b) Be _____ and _____.

Luke 4:18 (NIV): *The Spirit of the Lord is on me, because he has anointed me to preach good news to the poor. He has sent me to proclaim freedom for the prisoners and recovery of sight for the blind, to set the oppressed free.*

John 8:35-36 (NIV): *Now a slave has no permanent place in the family, but a son belongs to it forever. So if the Son sets you free, you will be free indeed.*

c) Be _____ and _____.

2 Corinthians 3:18 (MSG): *Our lives [are] gradually becoming brighter and more beautiful as God enters our lives and we become like him.*

Ephesians 4:7, 11-12 (NIV): *But to each one of us grace has been given as Christ apportioned it. . . . Christ himself gave the apostles, the prophets, the evangelists, the pastors and teachers, to equip his people for works of service.*

d) Be _____ and _____.

Ephesians 1:18-19 (NIV): *I pray that the eyes of your heart may be enlightened in order that you may know the hope to which he has called you, the riches of his glorious inheritance in his holy people, and his incomparably great power for us who believe.*

NOTES

Discuss

1. *How has God used your understanding of the four cups to strengthen your faith and encourage you on your journey?*

2. *Where do you presently see yourself on your spiritual journey? Where would you like to be? What do you need in order to get there?*

3. *Which of the four cups addresses your greatest need right now? Consider the following:*

   Cup 1 (Sanctification): freedom from slavery;
   Cup 2 (Deliverance): healing from our slavery mind-set;
   Cup 3 (Redemption): identity and purpose;
   Cup 4 (Praise): community and legacy.

4. *Rank the following from 1 to 9 (with 1 being most important) in order of what you think you need the*

most. Feel free to discuss your responses with other group members.

_____ Better understanding of your spiritual gifts

_____ Community (connection, fellowship, account-ability) with other believers

_____ A deeper, more trusting relationship with God

_____ More opportunities to serve others with your gifts

_____ A clearer sense of your God-given purpose

_____ New God-pleasing habits to replace your old mind-set and behavior

_____ Acceptance of Jesus as your Lord and Savior

_____ Daily encouragement to be who God made you to be

_____ Freedom from addictive habits and unhealthy thoughts

5. Write three action steps you can take to meet the above needs. Discuss with other group members to find encouragement and ideas for your action steps.

1.

2.

3.

Pray

Thank God for his promises and for the way he always meets you wherever you are on your spiritual journey. Share your needs with him, and trust him to provide all that you need. Lift up the needs of others in your group, and praise God for what he's doing in your lives. Conclude by asking God to direct you as you apply all that you've learned about him by studying his four cups of promise.

FOUR CUPS
RESOURCES

ANSWER KEY

Session 1

a) offer / guaranteed; b) know; c) understand; d) pursue

Session 2

a) salvation; b) deliverance; c) restoration; d) fulfillment

Session 3

a) perfect; b) sacrificed; c) shared

Session 4

a) Repent; b) Surrender; c) Relationship

Session 5

a) sin; b) wounds; c) enemy; d) Relationships

Session 6

a) Discover; b) Develop; c) Use; d) serve God / serving others

Session 7

a) calling; b) I want to; c) cause; d) Doing something;
e) me to we; f) With people; g) drink the final cup

Session 8

a) saved / set free; b) healed / delivered; c) discipled / equipped; d) empowered / fulfilled

MEMORY VERSES

SESSION 1

I praise your name for your unfailing love and faithfulness; for your promises are backed by all the honor of your name.

PSALM 138:2 (NLT)

SESSION 2

I am the LORD, and I will bring you out from under the yoke of the Egyptians. I will free you from being slaves to them, and I will redeem you with an outstretched arm and with mighty acts of judgment. I will take you as my own people, and I will be your God.

EXODUS 6:6-7 (NIV)

SESSION 3

All of God's promises have been fulfilled in Christ with a resounding "Yes!"

2 CORINTHIANS 1:20 (NLT)

SESSION 4

When the kindness and love of God our Savior appeared, he saved us, not because of righteous things we had done, but because of his mercy.

TITUS 3:4-5 (NIV)

SESSION 5

Who will free me from this life that is dominated by sin and death? Thank God! The answer is in Jesus Christ our Lord.

ROMANS 7:24-25 (NLT)

SESSION 6

For we are God's handiwork, created in Christ Jesus to do good works, which God prepared in advance for us to do.

EPHESIANS 2:10 (NIV)

SESSION 7

The thief's purpose is to steal, kill, and destroy. My purpose is to give life in all its fullness.

JOHN 10:10 (TLB)

SESSION 8

It's in Christ that we find out who we are and what we are living for. Long before we first heard of Christ and got our hopes up, he had his eye on us, had designs on us for glorious living, part of the overall purpose he is working out in everything and everyone.

EPHESIANS 1:11-12 (MSG)

HELP FOR HOSTS

Be sure you know the condition of your flocks, give careful attention to your herds.

PROVERBS 27:23 (NIV)

CONGRATULATIONS! You have responded to the call to help shepherd Jesus' flock. We are excited about what God is about to do in your life through this small-group experience. He is equipping you to do great things with him and for him. It is always those who step out to host a group who experience the greatest personal growth and blessing. Exciting and fulfilling days are ahead!

As you prepare to lead, here are a few thoughts to keep in mind:

1. Understand your role. Your primary role as a small-group leader is to assess the spiritual condition of your group members and help them move one step closer in their walk with Christ. If you can *encourage people, share Scripture, pray,* and *give next steps,* you can effectively lead a small group. Look up each of these Scriptures to equip

yourself with a shepherd's heart: Psalm 23, Ezekiel 34:11-16, and 1 Peter 5:2-4.

2. Be yourself. God wants to use your unique gifts and personality. Don't try to do things exactly like another leader; do them in a way that fits you. You don't have to pretend you have it all together. In fact, that doesn't help anybody. It's when we share from our weaknesses that we actually grow best. Remember, it is common for good leaders to feel as if they are not ready to lead. Moses, Solomon, Jeremiah, and Timothy were all reluctant leaders. Rely on God's promise in Hebrews 13:5 (NIV): "Never will I leave you; never will I forsake you." He will give you the wisdom, energy, stamina, and strength you need to do what you are called to do.

3. Don't do it alone. Ask God to help you build a healthy leadership team. If you can enlist a co-leader to help you with the group, you will find your experience to be much richer. Scripture tells us, "Two people are better off than one, for they can help each other succeed. If one person falls, the other can reach out and help" (Ecclesiastes 4:9-10, NLT). Many people are eager to help; they just need someone to ask them.

4. Prepare ahead of time. Invite the Holy Spirit to be a part of the group from the very start. Before each session, pray, preview the material,

and prepare your own heart to be real with your group. Remember, the goal isn't to go through all of the material but to build relationships in your group. Your job as a leader is not to have all of the answers but to help each member move one step closer to God and others in authentic relationship.

5. Pray for your group members. Prayer is the foundation for everything we do. "We have not stopped praying for you since we first heard about you. We ask God to give you complete knowledge of his will and to give you spiritual wisdom and understanding" (Colossians 1:9, NLT). Pray for your group members before you begin each session. Ask God to use your time together to touch the heart of each person uniquely. Review the prayer list between group meetings.

ABOUT CHRIS HODGES

CHRIS HODGES is the founding and senior pastor of Church of the Highlands, which has campuses all across the state of Alabama. Since it began in 2001, Church of the Highlands has experienced tremendous growth and is known for its life-giving culture and focus on leading people to an intimate relationship with God.

Pastor Chris has a deep passion for developing leaders and planting life-giving churches. In 2001, he cofounded ARC (Association of Related Churches), which has launched hundreds of churches all across America. He also founded a coaching network called GROW, which trains and equips pastors to help them break barriers and reach their growth potential. Chris is also the founder and president of Highlands College, a ministry training school that launches students into full-time ministry careers. Chris and his wife, Tammy, have five children and live in Birmingham, Alabama, where Church of the Highlands began. He speaks at conferences worldwide and is the author of *Fresh Air* and *Four Cups*.

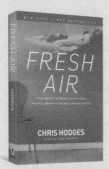